SY StorY

For Aladair Lane Scott
in the hope he will find a harbour
of his own

SY StorY

A PORTRAIT OF STORNOWAY HARBOUR

Donald S. Murray

ILLUSTRATIONS BY Douglas Robertson

BIRLINN

First published in Great Britain in 2015 by
Birlinn Ltd
West Newington House
10 Newington Road
Edinburgh
EH9 1QS

www.birlinn.co.uk

ISBN: 978 1 78027 260 3

British Library Cataloguing-in-Publication Data
A catalogue record for this book is available
from the British Library

Designed and typeset by Mark Blackadder

Printed and bound in Latvia by Livonia

Contents

An I-View   ix

A Wider Vantage   1

Beginnings   3
Herringopolis 1   4
The Ballad of the Fife Adventurers   6
Goat Island   7
Sprinkling Salt   9
Foreshores   10
Castle Grounds   13
Stirrings   15
Herringopolis 2   16
The Cooper's Song   17
The Herring Girl's Prayer   19
Love Song with Kippers   20
Horses   23
Stornoway Fishermen and Merchants   24
Spaces for the Shipwrecked   27
Chaie Wexler   29
Vlademar Gundel   32
Moishe Wexler   34
Rolf Vaagaasar   35
Photograph of *Norge* Survivors   37
Kristian Christensen   38

Love Song with Jelly Fish   39
Sea-shanty   40
Herring Girl in Love   41
Herring Girls in Wartime   43
Thomas F. Macleod   44
Iolaire   47
The *Iolaire* Memorial   48
Coal-hulk in Stornoway Harbour   49
Leverhulme   50
Metagama   53
Glitter   54
Stornoway in the Great Depression   55
Harbour Praise   56
Bela Lugosi in Stornoway   57
Psalm 46 in the Advent of War, 1939   58
Herring in Years of Conflict   61
Love Song with Whelks   62
The Arrival of the *Astrid*, 1948   65
James Cagney and Edward G. Robinson in Stornoway   67
Estonian Children on the *Astrid*   68
Operation Cauldron, 1952   70
A Fishy Story   78
Self-preservation   80
Marilyn Monroe in Stornoway   81
Tales My Uncle Told Me   82
Rudolf Nureyev in Stornoway   84
Lifting Light   85
Flooding   89
Below the Pier   90
Wool-sacks on the Harbour   93
A Meeting   94

Watching	95
Harbour Worker	96
Young Love in Stornoway	99
Old Love in Stornoway	100
Love Song with Dogfish	101
Love Song with Conger Eel	101
Dockers Strike, 1972	103
The Girl Who Taught the Fisherman To Read	104
Love Song without Sole	106
Love Song with Flounder	106
Unlucky Fisherman	107
Love Song with Crustaceans	111
Love Song with Seaweed	112
Love Song with Mackerel	113
Love Song with Sea Anemone	115
Sealessickness	116
In This Condition	117
At the Fish-mart	118
Leaving	120
Airnish	123
Love Song with Plankton	124
Love Song with Tropical Fish	125
Fishermen's Mission	126
A Short Selection of Announcements	127
Made by Cal Mac about the Failure of Their Vessel	
Isle of Lewis To Sail over the Last Few Years	
Boats	130
Love Song with Boats	131
Valediction	133
Rear View	135

An I-View

Many of my misspent teenage years were spent around Stornoway Harbour.

As hostel boys, adrift in town for much of the week as our homes were deemed to be too far from the main island school, the Nicolson Institute, to travel daily, we would wander round its quays throughout much of the early evening. In the course of this journey, we would perform our own native version of the Olympics, taking giant leaps across the fishing nets that lay sprawled on the harbour's edge, hurdling over bollards and chains in long-loped sprints, balancing on the pier as if we were testing gravity's ability to give us the slightest and smallest nudge. In our early years, as innocent twelve-year-olds, we would hide among the woolsacks that lay at the end of King Edward Wharf, imagining they were forts or sometimes diving boards. On other days, we would slip below the pier, exploring the world that existed in its shadows, occasionally 'shooting' at one of the other hostel lads who had also gone there in the twilight hours, clambering up and down each thick timber post that propped up the harbour. No doubt we even thumped our chests and performed Tarzan impersonations, our voices booming through that green and slithery world that existed below the edge of town.

Later on, of course, the harbour area was where I lost some of this innocence. A strange green, iron toilet that once stood there was where I sucked in the fumes of my first, second, third, fourth and fifth cigarettes, taking in the entire contents of a packet of five Woodbine in one sickening, toilet-filling gasp. After that, I graduated to the red-brick interior of the old Fisherman's Mart, where, despite the presence of a first cousin in the coal merchant, Duncan MacIver's office, I would risk my reputation's ruin in order to savour a cigarette during days when rain or hail drummed against the roof of that building. (There was much to love within that structure, especially the way our embryonic coughs would echo loud within.) Some years following this cloud-filled period in my existence, the downward process continued. I became an aficionado of fine wines, scrounging the occasional bottle of plonk from the crews on French or Spanish trawlers. It was from these gentlemen, too, that I also discovered the delights of French cigarettes, such as Disque Bleu or Gauloises, obtaining them free from the oil-stained hands of our Gallic neighbours, intent, perhaps, on corrupting the young Gaels they encountered on their voyages. It was, perhaps, this that led to the next stage of my development – the 'Oooh, la, la, mademoiselle!' I might have uttered when I walked arm in arm with some unfortunate young lady around the harbour. No doubt she was fooled by the air of suave sophistication I attempted to display while strutting on platform soles, wearing a crushed velvet jacket, Paisley pattern shirt and bell-bottom trousers. In the world of youthful romance, there are many flaws and failings that can be concealed by the scent of a bottle of Brut aftershave, including the reek of oil, grease and fish that – at this time – filled the harbour. Clearasil ruled, OK!

Yet even these heady smells did not obscure the main business of the harbour. That bustled all around us. Even before many of my age-group were marooned in the hostel and still lived in the infinitely more civilised confines of Ness, there were evenings when we would travel across to town to meet relatives arriving on the *Loch Seaforth*, skippered at that time by John Smith, a native of my home village of South Dell. This rather loose local connection helped me to claim some kind of ownership of the various visions that were on display on King Edward Wharf. They included the vehicles swinging like slow pendulums as they were lowered onto land, the gangway being clinked and clattered into place, but most of all, there was the sheer number of people who thronged the harbour. Those who lived near the centre of town would even forsake the delights of *Z-Cars* or *The Man from U.N.C.L.E.* to go down and see the *Seaforth* dock – a choice unimaginable to us country lads, who often did not even have the sinful pleasure of having a TV in our homes.

And then there was the day when that moment was altered, when the concrete posts were embedded in the sea and a stretch of tarmac could be seen hovering over water. Our eyes soon opened to another wonder. We left the hostel to see the *Suilven* arrive in port, its mouth opening to allow a stream of cars to escape from its throat. It was a change we marvelled at, comparing it in our minds to that uneasy balance by which Hillman Hunters and Sunbeams arrived in Stornoway just a short time before. We were witnesses to a miracle, the open sea merging with the open road. No longer did people sometimes have to travel twisting tracks of tar or rail to Kyle of Lochalsh – past Dornie, perhaps, or the stony gaze of the men immortalised in the Commando Memorial near Spean Bridge. Instead, we journeyed out the length of Loch Broom, past the Summer Isles, knowing our cars were safe in the belly of the beast, without any grim expectation of that moment when they swung and swayed above our heads, fearing that there might suddenly be a slip between quay and ship. It was a change that brought about the 'disappearance' of the dockers, those who occupied the small building where Norman MacArthur (or 'Brot') from Carloway holds court today, his views and opinions clear from the posters and notices that decorate the room. (Suffice it to say that Rangers FC is the only team in town.) Once, though, a hundred dockers spent their hours here, bustling around the piers. Shortly after the arrival of the *Suilven,* there were only twenty.

Yet in addition to these men and their trade, there were the fishing boats that thronged the harbour. Some bore girls' names, like *Catriona* or *Girl Norma,* recalling, perhaps, some of the young ladies we tried to woo on a stroll around the quay. Others seemed precious in other ways like the *Amethyst* or *Sapphire,* an attempt, perhaps, to transform their wooden hulls into sparkling gems. There were also the obscure – such as *Quo Vadis,* conjuring up the image of a Roman general in, say, the film of *Spartacus* interrogating the fishermen on the deck, or *Mizpah* with its reference to one of the more esoteric and mysterious parts of the Bible. The *Comrade* offered a revolutionary message. One could almost expect Lenin or Karl Marx to be among its crew, a red flag waving from the cabin when a full harvest of fish arrived in its hold. In contrast, the *Astronaut* brought to mind another day a flag fluttered – when Messrs Armstrong and Aldrin stepped onto the surface of the moon, the banner of the greatest running dog of capitalism fluttering alongside their luminous, floating forms.

As a Nessman, from the island's northern end, we would sometimes stop and talk to those from our district working on boats called the *Calina, Islesman, Rona* and *Alpha* – much more plain and less pretentious than those who breathed in the heady air of the peninsula of Point and gave their vessels such names as *Providence* and *Perseverance.* These Niseach boats bore family friends and relatives both among my own folk and those of my mates from the hostel. Sometimes too, especially on a Friday evening when we were heading home on the bus, we would be given a plastic bag full of fish to take home to our parents for a 'fry'. As someone who also had cousins in Tolsta, I would occasionally be given a little of the catch from their boats too; a gift to a distant relative who had flown (by whatever means!) across the moor.

It was in that way we came to know the harbour, recognising the men who auctioned fish in the Mart, their voices pitching ever more highly as the price went up, the fishermen appraising the merit of the catch as the count went on, shaking heads and muttering to themselves. There were others, too, whom we came to know in other ways – the town's local characters who often spent as many hours as we did wandering the quay. Alert to any real or imagined peculiarities, we spotted a bald-headed individual whom we alternately mocked and indulged. Noting the way his trousers hung loosely around his waist, the shuffle of his feet, we would sometimes treat him to a bag of chips in either of the town's fast-food establishments. There was another slight individual who was dwarfed by his large gaudy-coloured motorbike. The sight of his squashed nose should have been enough to let us know he had been a fly-weight boxer in his early life. However, this did not prevent some of us teasing him, even once placing a banger in the exhaust of his celebrated vehicle. Both the man's temper and his motor-bike exploded almost simultaneously after that.

And then there were the individuals who frequented one of the other cultural high-points of the town. Variously called the 'Opera House' or 'Lemen' (after the 'Gent' part of its title had slipped off), the late and unlamented men's toilets in Perceval Square was the place where long renditions of Gaelic songs could be heard, booming from throats long lubricated by cans of McEwans or half-bottles of Dewar's whisky. It was a venue and repertoire disapproved of by the cailleachs (or old ladies) of the town, whose heels and tongues would click in disapproval as they made their way to church in Kenneth Street or Matheson Road, walking as quickly out of range of the various raucous melodies as was humanly possible.

It was also a location where we gained an awareness of other sounds and music, such as the peal of gulls following a fishing boat into harbour, squealing out for their own small allotment of man's huge catches of fish. On the opposite side of harbour, in a shallow stretch of water, a heron often stood, its eye and beak poised to pin down the glitter of scales, the swift movement of fins. Its sharp-eyed gaze was almost matched by Sammy the one-eyed seal who swam around the bay, fixing his disconcerting glare upon all passers-by in the hope that, like a number of the fishermen, they might also seek to provide him with an added layer of blubber by feeding him some of their fish and chips

I gained much of my love of wildlife from strolling around the harbour, seeing small, unusual birds in the trees and bushes of the Castle Grounds, hearing the ominous calls of crows greeting young lovers as they strolled below the trunks and branches Sir James Matheson had set down there in the latter years of the nineteenth century. There were many joys to be found in that distinct and unusual landscape on what was otherwise bare land – not all, I have to say, connected with the young lady who had the bad judgement to walk by your side.

Then there were our heroes – those who volunteered for lifeboat duty to save the lives of 'those in peril on the sea'. Even today, I am still a little in awe of them, recalling the mingling of excitement and terror that ran through us when the bright flare of a rocket could be seen through the glass of the hostel window, its light bursting over the Castle Grounds or the streets of the town. In that week's *Gazette,* we would read of the various rescues that had occurred – the black print smearing our fingers as we took in each dramatic detail of the incident which we had imagined occurring in the darkness. These moments brought men from exotic ports and other places to our shores. There would be snapshots of Italians, Portuguese and Spanish sailors in the pages of both local newspapers and – sometimes – even the national press. Sometimes, too, there would be tales of tragedy, the rescues which – despite the efforts of our local volunteers – had failed to save lives.

For all its smallness, this made Stornoway a far less parochial place than many inland and far larger towns. It was, in some ways, a global classroom – a tradition that still continues with the yachts that nowadays visit the harbour, their exotic places of origin painted in dark letters upon steel. Back then Faroese fishermen wandered through the streets of the town; one of them even once inexplicably offered me a bag of grapes on the part of the Harbour we called Lazy Corner – an act of kindness I have never quite forgotten. I recall a German sailing ship tying up at King Edward Wharf too, its crew offering the chance to the entire school-roll of the Nicolson Institute to clamber over its decks. And there was even, in the days before Gorbachev, Perestroika and Glasnost, shipfuls of Russian sailors congregating in the town. Occasionally, if you looked carefully, you could catch a cheerful glint in the eye of one, a sign that, in the words of the rock-star Sting, 'Russians loved their children' – and perhaps even troubled teenagers too.

All this added to the linguistic mix that was to be found in the town. Along with Gaelic, there were sometimes bracing gusts of German and Norwegian blowing through the town shops, such as Woolworths or one of the two chemists on Cromwell Street. There were probably days when the rhythms of Italian and Spanish could be heard in Murdo Maclean's where the men were no doubt flummoxed by the sheer array of communion hats on display. (For all that southern talk of Gucci, flamenco-dancing and *la dolce vita,* one can only be certain that they were impressed by the sheer range of headgear – all designed for the pretty *signorita* or *senorita* back home.) The voices of the French also swirled around King Edward Wharf too, fending off the many requests for wine and cigarettes I made in my sinful, smoke-filled past.

It is a tradition that, as I have noted, still continues. Walking around the harbour once again this week, I was conscious that the men who worked the fishing boats were sometimes very different from those I had seen twenty-odd years before, but much was similar too. Men from far outside the islands were stitching a green fishing net, drawing a needle through its web, making sure each inch was secure in much the same way as the crew of the *Calina* and *Alpha* had done when I talked to them these years before. A stitch in the weave that makes up our modern existence, they also showed us how life in Stornoway has been part of an ever-changing tradition, a 'flowing stream' to borrow the name of a vessel connected to the town. It is a story that contains the hunter-gatherers that used to frequent these islands, Viking raiders, Cromwell's men, the *Iolaire* and the *Metagama*, the Fife Adventurers and Lord Leverhulme. It is one that, largely connected by the sea, I have attempted to tell in the words that follow, employing the skills that – hopefully! – I have acquired during my teenage years around Stornoway Harbour and my time as a writer today. Finally, it is also often informed by myth, particularly about the life of the early history of the town. Were three stones – found in Gallows Hill, Garrabost and Broadbay – used to guide the hunter-gatherers of the Mesolithic era into the bay? Was Cromwell's garrison on Goat Island or elsewhere? There are some questions to which we may never have a definitive answer. The evidence as to whether Cromwell's fort ever existed was cleared away many years ago when the island's surface was flattened and a causeway built to its shores.

In short, this is my personal history of Stornoway – with all the flaws and errors that are always present in one person's limited view. It owes much to Catherine Mackay's wonderfully informative book, *It Must Be Stornoway*, but also a great deal to my own imagination. As such I hope at least that it is always informative and entertaining, as much myth and fable as a tale cabined and confined, cramped and constricted by detailed historic research.

I hope it is in this spirit that you – as reader – come to the book that lies open before you.

Speedwell, old comrade, let the wavecrest take you through . . .

Donald S. Murray
December 2014

A Wider Vantage

Beginnings

The town's beginnings lay
within a triangle of stones
 – on Garrabost, Gallows Hill, Broadbay –
glimpsed on the horizon
by Mesolithic wanderers who came
to make their temporary home
on this shoreline, sparking flame,
seeking water, localities they could roam
and find sustenance, granting places names
now forgotten and unknown,

Yet the essence of their untamed
spirits are still within the waters when sea-foam's
stirred on its surface, when frenzied winds reclaim
the moorland, the fierce nights we are shown
our foundations here are fragile,
when our tongues can be shamed
into confessing there is ground here
no man can claim to own.

Herringopolis 1

When jarls looked out for shelter from the winter,
they had in mind a place like this
with land that curled around the harbour
walling off the ocean's turbulence,
fresh water, too, that graced their lips
with the sweetness of a woman's kiss,
the solace of flat land where men could plough
or dig the deep foundations of a northern metropolis.

Or they might have seen a vision of a crowded bay with
    smacks,
and schooners jostling at anchor; fishermen and fishwives
singing Gaelic songs, sea-shanties, as they bowed backs
heaving herring-barrels, sliding gutting-knives
like needles trailing thread
through tails and fins and gills
that glittered, shone and shimmered
in the dim light of that northern metropolis.

Or perhaps they witnessed container-lorries, cranes
rattling chains around the harbour
or the skitter of sea-scales that remain
once a buyer's order is paid for,
seeing those who brought that catch to shore
as ghosts, translucent, luminous,
legacies of ones who sailed here years before
to found this northern metropolis.

The Ballad of the
Fife Adventurers

O gin that ma Rob was still here,
nae lying in cauld clay
or ablow the green waves that must sough
o'er his banes near Stornoway,

For it wis tae these northern airts
that he and vessel both set sail,
commanded there by Jamie Saxt
to force the heathens there to hail

Him king and pit their lives in thrall
tae the Lallans, God and law,
but insteid these pagans drew their swords
and hacked guid men in pieces sma'.

Amang them Rob wha lies amang
the cauld, cauld clay or bitter waves.
O gin he were here, here in my bed
and nae in a grave near Stornoway,

For the wind blaws fierce o'er Fife,
its chill still haunts my day
I greet an' mourn the luve I lost
wha set his sail for Stornoway.

Goat Island

We heard the clamour of it,
hammers clanging a hull's armour
spilling round the bay,
the welding rods, helmets and visors
recalling to us the sentries
that back in Cromwell's day
patrolled this island. A fort stood here
once lit by brands of wax or seal-fat,
but now dark's eased by streetlight
or where the breach within a trawler's keel
is healed by an oxy-acetylene spark.
And there is, too, a rattle
as white-suited, green-booted women
bear cold skeletons of prawns.
Close your eyes. Imagine it,
how old soldiers linger on,
the ghosts of the Protector's men never, ever gone.

Sprinkling Salt

If love preserves us,
it must be like this
with countless pinpricks of light,
a filigree of kisses,
swarm of sparks
that gleam and glitter in that dark
into which the mere fact
of being human sometimes sends us,
that swift descent
into the hold of night
till we are lifted whole and upright
by a smattering of brightness,
a thousand tiny beams that glow
and thaw ice layered deep within us,
a static charge
with power beyond comprehension,
that could heal the world we live in
and raise the universe.

Foreshores

Like gulls, they squabbled
for control of foreshores,
disputing rights to pebbles,
casting gneiss-hard glowers
on those who stepped in the direction
of their individual crops of stones.

Every boulder quarrelled over as they claimed
each strand of kelp
washed up by wave,
those stacks of shingle swept
broad and tall by squalls
to form territorial limits, walls

On which these birds would strut, parade,
proclaim rights of ownership
of all the Minch has left within its wake,
tear bites and strips
of debris that the ocean has let slip,
gorging on what profits either time or tide can make.

Castle Grounds

There would have been men and women
who journeyed from the country
to witness trees
the rich man had allegedly set down
on the salt edge of town,

And wondered at them,
these brown trunks of kelp
that helped to keep
storms at bay from buildings
or were set as bulwarks against tides
that sought to shift all trace
of soil and boulders
from the places
where men dug these roots down,

And, too, that surge of green
that spring in its full spate would bring
each year to the tangle
that his lordship
set high above the ground,

The birds slipping among branches
like plovers zig-zagging
through twists of sea-wrack
before the ocean's stretching out and turning back,
sprinkling heights with tiny tracks of sound.

Stirrings

No wonder we grew restless
with earth in gardens ballast from Spain
becoming engrained in our feet.
Kenneth Street containing
particles of Poland,
while the huge sweep of the Russian steppes
kept that shoreline in a tight hold
no matter how the oceans swept
up to wear its thin grip down.
And, of course, French soil fed trees
green within the Castle Grounds.
Small marvel then we found
so many of us left these quays
to find out foreign parts,
that soil grounded deep within us
lavish cargo for the human heart.

Herringopolis 2

Preserved by the salt gravel, the cold smack of sea
would be kept within stout barrels on the pier
till a blizzard brewed inside wood, spilling free
from hoop and stave; the cooper's craft no barrier

For the way that flakes could seep from birch or fir
in a sudden smirr of silver, a hail of scales, coarse grains
that settled down on Point Street, brought winter
back again to fish-buyer and herring girl,
    all whose clothes were stained

By work upon that trade, till the whole town grew still
below the frozen air of oceans, the chill
shuddering through the island's fishermen
these moments when their boats and nets strained full.

The Cooper's Song

The cooper bound his chest with iron bands
when he thought his love was lost,
sailing off to Wick or Yarmouth
or some distant eastern coast.
The cooper bound his chest with iron bands
for fear his heart might burst.

The cooper bound his chest with iron bands
till the morning that he learned
she was sailing back to him,
a little cash to earn.
The cooper bound his chest with iron bands
till the morning she returned.

The cooper bound his chest with iron bands
till her kiss brought release;
the snapping of each loop and bolt
a bringing of relief.
The cooper bound his chest with iron bands
till her grace delivered peace.

The Herring Girl's Prayer

Lord, protect me from the blade I wield.
shield me from any rise or dip
that might slip and cut my hands,

And spare me, too, from salt that smarts
open wounds, coarse grains that grind
into a gash or bruise,
digging deep into my hands
for sometimes, blisters weep,
betraying me
on this icy edge of land.

Love Song with Kippers

Let us meet inside the smokehouse
where we will not sense the shame
with which some will try to douse our love,
snuff out its spark and flame.

Let us meet inside the smokehouse
and not surrender to the fear
that one day this will all be over,
become marinated with our tears.

Let us meet inside the smokehouse
for love is bright and burnished there,
salted by the scent of danger,
given added savour by our cares.

Let us meet inside the smokehouse
knowing we will greet within
a love hooking deep inside us,
its heat scorching our skin.

Fishing Season at Stornoway

Horses

The grey mares of the klondyke years
spent the season within shafts
weighed down with barrels,
drinking down chill draughts
of water to slake and take away the thirst
that salt, dry oats had cursed them with,
abating the loud whinny that stayed fixed within their throats.

2

An old mare's flank and tail
glistened with so many scales
that one day coopers saw a change begin
within her. First, the mane and fetlocks altered,
transforming into fins,
its grey neck gaining gills
until the hour she seemed to have her fill
of land, leaping into water,
beginning first to swim
towards Goat Island and Airnish, and then inch by inch
a slow and steady canter out across the Minch.

The other horses trembled before their carts
and watched her taking leave,
wondering how much salt and herring they might have to heave
before they could jump into the harbour,
find air enough to breathe.

Stornoway Fishermen and Merchants

(circa 1900)

Did these men have an inkling
these days would not last,
their sons no longer able to stand upright
before a thick woodland of masts

shadowing the harbour,
and, too, their sons might hack
hull and keel for firewood,
split the mizzen with an axe?

Or that their sons would leave
these quays to be
foresters' apprentices,
cut branches, trunks of trees?

Or else plant seeds in prairie soil,
reap and harvest, discover how
to open up a dark wake on the earth
with the steel keel of a plough?

Spaces for the Shipwrecked

They opened homes to unexpected guests
thrown upon their kindness by the ocean's surge,
inviting castaways among them to share meals prepared
for hunger-scavenged households, aware that they had less
because of those who scrambled from the *Annie Jane*
 or *Norge*
or some other ship that floundered to these islands'
  east or west.

In return, those travellers granted voices – melodies for ears
long restricted to those simple tongues they knew.
A dark, Italian tenor lulls to sleep a restless girl
with an aria that echoes throughout her adult years,
while a Presbyterian minister sits beside a Polish Jew,
discerning signs that the Messiah's time may soon be
  drawing near.

And they talk of America – that bright and spangled state
where a statue stretches out for huddled souls;
a medley of peoples in which Danes, Russians, Poles
might pray for new beginnings, escaping the dark fates
that drove them out of Europe, fleeing the control
of Tsars or small town bullies who despised them for
  their faith.

Yet among them were emigrants dispatched to the quiet
corners of a graveyard. Below their granite monuments
the unknown dead lie boxed or stitched within a shroud.
They set out in hope from harbours, only to alight
upon an edge of croftland, places no one went
except when misfortune drove them, urged on by the tide.

And this was their finality. A rock's grating
against steel halting planned excursions within wide,
      sky-scrapered streets.
Or storm or squall that swirled some down into the deep,
settling others here among us, hosted inside graves
secure and walled in cemeteries or where the machair's sweep
is ended and eroded – just like their lives – by waves.

Chaie Wexler

(passenger on the *Norge*, sunk off Rockall, 28 June 1904)

In her life, there was no desolation greater
than her razed town, the burnt and desecrated synagogue
till that moment when a concealed rock
chafed the great hull of the *Norge*.

That instant shuddered through her, while lifeboats
                                    were jerked
down into water; one man leapt from deck,
to break a leg; a sudden jolt as that ship floundered, wrecked
near Rockall, plunging in a bed of skerries, bladderwrack
                                    and kelp.

Yet there were other moments, long after she was drenched
upon that lifeboat, when her fellow-Jews stretched
arms to tug unfamiliar oars; when she could sense the stench
of death about them till that moment they were wrenched

to safety, to the boat that carried them to shore
where she lay grateful for a cabin bed, the half-jammed door
behind which she could hold her children and implore
God not to take them, not like that other child whose
                                    body was already stored

fathoms-deep. *'Moishe, Israel, Meir . . .'*
she chanted out their names, as if each word was a prayer
she could cling onto like fingers, till that instant on the pier
when the clasp was broken. No longer there,

she screamed out for them, haunting the hospital with calls
misunderstood by nurses, a babble
echoing in Yiddish, till a doctor recognised that within
                                                    poorhouse walls
there were children who looked like her, who squalled

out, too, in terror. So he set them in each other's arms,
the phrases *'Shalom . . . A sheynem dank'* bringing hush
                                                    to their alarm.

Vlademar Gundel
(captain of the *Norge*)

I possessed no sextant, chart
and could only navigate
because some Jew became aware of this
constant tick around his heart.

He fished out a pocket-watch he'd bought
from a pocket at his chest,
one that stored a compass
allowing me to distinguish east from west.

And too there were the night skies,
the steady gleam of stars,
how constellations inclined
from the perpendicular.

It allowed me to forget
for a short time, the sudden scrape
that jolted through me,
the scene of my disgrace,

clutching handrails,
stumbling from the bridge,
captain's coat torn at the shoulders
in my desperate efforts to escape.

Moishe Wexler

(son of Chaie and passenger on the *Norge*)

Sometimes he saw shadows of that rock
in the tenements of his new home in New York,

those who came from distant edges of the world
shrieking like the bedlam of these gulls

watching them from granite ledges,
scolding Captain Gundel's absence from the bridge

the instant when stone ground keel and bow.
And, too, there was that time on the lifeboat – how

Jew and Scandinavian rowed to land,
their differences forgotten in the rhythm and grip of hands

till they reached the shelter of the shore.
Then once more they were deafened, the uproar

of Gaelic, English voices, how arms rushed to embrace
the sick and dying, never questioning their race

or nation, living witness of what he came to understand
was the kith and kinship of the ordinary man.

Rolf Vaagaasar

(survivor of the *Norge*)

Out of where passageways pressed down on me,
the crashing deck, ripped windows,
ice-black water, smashed fo'c'sle,
there seemed no place that I could race and go

to break free from that carnage;
it stays with me in Lom
among the mountains, the peace of church,
the grain and straw of farms

I till and plough, the memory of that moment
I bowed and cupped my hands to lift up
sea-water, how I screamed and others lashed me to the gunnels,
the madness of that brew my broken lips had supped.

Photograph of *Norge* Survivors
(outside the Poorhouse, Stornoway)

Local tailors gave them caps to kit
them for the stern pose a photograph entailed
back in those days. Dresses, suits, too, to make them fit
for this public portrayal.

And so they sit or stand, freshly buttoned, braced
for the camera and shutter to be set,
the glare of flash upon each staring face
as an inch of powder's lit,

trying their best to leave all thought
of that day they arrived in this small town
with both friends and luggage lost
as that long deck tilted and slid down.

Kristian Christensen
(survivor of the *Norge*)

Nothing seemed to nail me down
to my new life in the new world.

Not the railroad sleepers, cross-ties, rails,
I toiled over in that workshop
in Carbondale, Pennsylvania.

So I went home without complaint,
picked up my father's trade and pails of paint,
left dark dreams behind,

going home to Laasby,
varnishing darkness from thought,
brushing memories clean out of my mind.

Love Song with Jelly Fish

When we come across one,
it is all washed up,

an amethyst among flotsam,
a pale flickering

that slipped the grip
of seaweed

and now lies stranded
upon a bank of sand,

and we can only picture
it opening and closing,

how it swirls and tilts
while it skirts the sea's entanglements,

as hard to grasp and capture
as what often eludes us

when deep within its element
we might glimpse

the unfathomable stirrings
that shift the human heart.

Sea-shanty

It wasn't the wind so much as a knock
that frightened them on nights of storms,
the tap on a door that rattled, unlocked,
during these hours their men were gone
out on boats that tipped and rocked
in open seas, wide bays, sea-lochs.

It wasn't the wind so much as its moan
that caused them dread as they perched over flames,
seeking to bring fire back to their bones
and praying to God that nobody came
with dark intimations to their home
and tell them tomorrow they'd lie all alone.

It wasn't the wind so much as the sparks
of doubt spitting through minds on nights like these,
the fear that kelp and bladder-wrack
might twist round lamp-posts, drape on quays
with the wreckage of schooners, drifters, smacks
compelling the grieving to search through the dark.

Herring Girl in Love

Sometimes the thought still shook her;
a cold smattering of hail,
certain shade of wool,
both recalled that fisherman from Lubeck or Kiel
whose presence had first thrilled her
when he hoisted high that barrel
her deft hands had stacked and filled.

She longed for his survival.
Even on the day her brothers
put on service uniforms
and headed out to kill
those who were his kind and kin,
she prayed that either wind or wave could still
bullets fired in his direction,
faster than the silver fins
of shoals his wide, strong shoulders
heaved and hauled within
the vessel coming into harbour,
bringing together, briefly, her and him.

She hoped he'd soon come back to her,
step dry and whole into her world,
and she might draw him to her
by a slight slip of her shawl,
a shy revealing smile or curl of hair
how glad he was to see him
among both boats and barrels there.

Herring Girls in Wartime

1

Herring used to shoal upon the town;
a tumble of silver coming down
and mingling with the ring of roubles, guilders, Danish krone

on the heads of herring girls and curers on South Beach quay,
who dipped their hands in barrels to lift the currency
of Empires, that splendid legacy of seas

that showered on cement and concrete till the deluge stilled
and men sailed out on ships to spill
the blood of an entire continent, employing gutting
    knives and bayonets,

whatever blades their hands could find
to maim and wound and kill.

2

In these years, they scrubbed clean
entrails and scales that clung to hands
to gain a grip on weapons that they fashioned
to maim and kill and rip the guts out of their fellow man.

Thomas F. Macleod
(1869–1960)

(From Stornoway, MacLeod took part in three Antarctic expeditions – accompanying Scott in 1910 and Shackleton in both 1914 and 1920. Credited with being the individual who suggested building a cairn to mark the latter's grave in South Georgia, he claimed to owe nothing to either Lewis or Scotland.)

Deny it if you can – and yet these stones
picked up to place on Shackleton's remains
revealed how much of the island was contained
within the frozen marrow of your bones.

That cairn's foundation a thought recalled
from days exploring moor and shore.
These grey, lichen-spangled towers
bare pinnacles on hill-tops; shadowing a lochside; all
landmarks layers of Lewisian gneiss
ancestors stacked and lodged to stand
to leave us puzzling over what purpose they were planned,
what event was marked there we no longer recognised.

Deny it if you can – and yet that Bible too
you reclaimed after Shackleton tossed its weight aside,
as if God's voice had no meaning among the snow and ice,
showed how much the island still remained in you.

46

Iolaire

Sometimes we still sit upon that ledge
and consider the dark fervour of the waves,
wondering why some of us went under
while others clung with every fibre and were saved.
There are no answers to that question. Fortune
(whatever scholars tell us) does not favour the brave
or the virtuous. It rescued some
who could be wicked, hard and wretched ones enslaved
to drink or women, and swept aside
the good, the kind, those who each day forgave
others. We only know a rope was hurled
and we possessed both grip and faith
strong enough to hold it. Nothing else is known to us,
all as dark, intangible as the fervour of these waves.

The *Iolaire* Memorial

We wanted to forget them,
avoid all mention of their loss,
let them slip into a dark void
and not think of the storm-tossed
waves that night, knowing our dreams
were still haunted by their cries of desperation,
each unheard shout and scream.

And so we built this small
reminder on the headland,
one dwarfed by the light
of that stone tower outside town
marking those who died on dry land
or, perhaps, been swatted from the skies or drowned,
but elsewhere, far from these shores,
an act of self-deception,
by which we could somehow pretend
their days had never ended,
that both the darkness and our deafness
had never, ever been.

Coal-hulk in Stornoway Harbour

Coals from Newcastle or Ayrshire were brought
to harbour in creaking boats
which men would look at, wonder
how they stayed afloat and never foundered
with the weight of dark rocks
ferried to an island
waterlogged by lochs and bogs,
covered by the peat that each year
fathers travelled out to harvest,
stripped and dug.

So far removed from diamonds
that fuel they spent the summer mining,
they would look at chunks and chips of coal
as if each was a ruby shining
long before the fire transformed
it with the glow of flame and heat,
hoping that if men dug down deep enough,
there would be sparkling jewels
beneath the turf that stretched below our feet.

Leverhulme

And we watched him stand upon the Town Hall stage,
his hands transform a powder-puff of soap-flakes
    into fish-scales,
tiny silver flecks of skin and fin he'd unfurl with
    his fingers. Then he would begin
unfurling nets out of a top-hat, creating waves
    and shaping wings
with gestures that danced so high above our heads,
all thought reeled with the magic of what he did and said.
For those who sat applauding, bowing to the spell
of the soap-king and his bubbles, the rise and swell
of words sparkling through the air that night
was an abracadabra, hey presto that gave this
    port sunlight . . .

Until his stage act vanished and we could see a joke
had been played upon us, his promises illusions,
    a sudden puff of smoke.

Metagama

When we watched our children leaving, fighting tears,
Calum spoke of the ruin that lay below the pier,
Nicol Hasson's fort that once marked the frontier

Of a northern warrior's ground, a citadel
(long after) overcome and felled by Cromwell
with its walls still hefted by the swell

Of water. Both lost worlds. Just like sagas told
of *Stjornavager*, tales of bard or skald
of raids and killingfests, hearts as harsh and cold

As permafrost our exiled young
might be sailing out to step upon
to go and tell some Northern sagas they could
    make all their own.

Glitter

In daylight, that pier
stretched out like a table-top
which at evening's end was washed and cleared.

At night, the moonlit sky
soaking up spare silver,
the sprinkling of change, too, the herring girls set by.

Stornoway in the Great Depression

Drift-nets have a thousand eyes
with which busy fishermen could look
daily at the idle strolling down the pier
and bait their path with jibes and hooks

cast in their direction,
wounding men who'd slipped the lines
that hauled up others,
impaling them for having time

to walk past fishing boats
sharing jokes with herring girls
in exchange for thin throatfuls
of laughter, the skirl

of merriment. It was always thus.
The workless mocked by those who work
for having time to walk that empty-bellied path,
the endless stretch from dawn's first gleam to dusk.

Harbour Praise

Crops of salt-burnt oats or bere
made thin and paltry bread to share
among congregations in the harbour
when they bowed heads in prayer,

but they would sometimes bring
fragments of herring, coalfish, ling
to grant savour to their voices
when they opened lips to sing

psalms, share potatoes, too, to fill
their hollow bellies and allow God's praise to swirl
around the waters of that bay;
a reprise of the miracle

when Christ lifted up what men had reaped
from earth and sea
to share among those gathered
on the shores of Galilee.

Bela Lugosi in Stornoway

I was definitely typed, doomed
to be an exponent of evil:
each time I stepped into a room,
there was that still
expectation something wicked would be done,
until within the murk of winter,
without beam or glint of sun,
I found that kirk and entered
a hall where black coats clustered,
dark funereal hats loomed over pews,
and this old preacher in the pulpit mustered
just about enough strength to give the news
that human souls could rise again without the need
to bleed others dry and white.
I felt my cloak shrug off me then,
no longer seeking refuge within the gloom of night.

Psalm 46 in the Advent of War, 1939

'Come and behold what wondrous works
have by the Lord been wrought.
Come, see what desolation
He on the earth hath brought.'
The young man in starched uniform
wrapped within his thoughts.
The older man recalling
the last time legions fought,

And how they, too, once gathered
in crowds upon this pier,
from Kirk, workplace and crofthouse
to this building where
this sheltered bay is washed by psalm,
the cold breeze softened by a prayer
to help men stand and carry arms
that – for generations– they've been forced to bear

And so their voices ripple across harbour
from the vessel's bow and stern,
as they echo that faint promise
they hope power will one day learn.
'Unto the ends of all the earth,
War into peace He turns.
The bow He breaks, the spear He cuts
In fire the chariot burns.'

Herring in Years of Conflict

No shoals around these shores in 1939,
as if the quick heads of herring had divined
that the men who fished for them would not be inclined

to go out in these waters, aware storms were about to break
over Minch and Atlantic, other vessels come to take
possession of these currents with fish departing in the wake

of warships, making way for steel instead,
depth charges and torpedoes, men sailing there to net
a steady haul and harvest of the wounded and the dead.

Love Song with Whelks

For Maree Morrison (Reading), Mairi Morrison (Cross), Mary 'Ryno' Morrison, Mairi Morrison (artist, Shader), Mary 'Ruchdaidh' Morrison, Mary . . .

Went out to the whelks last night with Mary Morrison.
Came back with a sackful.
Watched her fingers dip and scoop,
scrambling through rockpools
for shells that glittered in her pail.
She rarely spoke about her life
apart from saying that the tide had long gone out.
Took this to mean she'd never be a wife
or had been crossed in love,
that the only silver glinting
on her hand would be scales and gills of herring.
Yet despite this, she still holds and clings
like limpets to these rocks, defying all the tide might bring
round to dislodge her. Oh, though other girls are fair and braw
and rarely seen in wellingtons,
there's no doubt the fairest of them a',
the lovely Mary Morrison.

The Arrival of the *Astrid*, 1948

You'd thought of that tribe
as those who'd fled Egypt,
their boat breaking paths through waves
similar to Moses who, raising his staff,
had cleaved passage for the enslaved
through the Red Sea
to where they might be safe.

On board, their meagre store.
Not like Joseph who had shored
a state against starvation
with hoards of fruit and grain.

Little remained
of all they'd gained and bartered
weeks before they decided
they could no longer stay
on land fit only for husks and chaff
where the threat of Arctic wind
had blown good seed away.

And so they'd set off to flee the plague and storm
that had settled on their homeland,
the curse on the first and second born
that brought them to this bay,

risking storm and seas to slip away
from the barbed camp of a Pharaoh,
unwilling to experience what they had seen so long before,
their fallow years of want and isolation any more.

James Cagney and
Edward G. Robinson in Stornoway

They would leave the soft fedoras
that lined and creased the steep crags of their brows
on a pew or window,
so they might be allowed to bow

bare heads towards the Big Boss,
acknowledging a God
they clothed with their sharp certainties,
all square-shouldered suit and polished shoes,
    accompanied by a squad

of angels kitted out in black or pinstripe,
mouth rattling verse and catechism against rebellious souls
who dared to stand against them, defying prohibition
by supping down hard liquor, skipping through the Boston
    Two Step, slipping all control . . .

Estonian Children
on the *Astrid*

The children whisper
of their parents' hope
that one day winter
will melt away,

its shadows dwindling
like these long-coated men
who stand above them
on the quay,

as those who guarded
ocean in their homeland,
halted sail and oar
when rays

of daylight had receded,
halting them from setting foot
on rock or sand
or setting out to sea

in dark or twilight
to dip nets deep in water,
each line barbed like the gulag-wire
that stopped their nation swimming free.

Operation Cauldron, 1952

1

The seas were haunted by them.
The jabbering of macaques mimicked by grey seals.
Cuddies stout as guinea pigs
racing in a frenzy round a wheel.
The entire ocean bubbling
with a foul concoction sprayed
by wizards on that boat.
'A quick dash of bubonic plague.
Swift brush of brucellosis.
Splash of rabbit fever inhaled
by these creatures trapped within a cage . . .'

And, too, the *Carella* sailing near
that pontoon where poison breath
festered, trailing nets through mists and shoals
tainted by black death.

2

He plagued her at that town-hall dance,
stumbling in her footsteps throughout an eightsome reel,
prowling round her in a quickstep
while talking in that Geordie accent about love,
      Ben Lomond and romance.

She ignored him, especially when he spoke of all his worries,
of how he had a monkey on his shoulder
chattering away at him, how he was haunted
by their cries and voices. She brushed away his cares,
      made out she was in a hurry

to meet her pals. Later she found
he'd been arrested, lifted by a constable for
      trying to steal a car
and get away from these parts. She was not surprised;
that strangeness so apparent when he tried to
      speak above the sound

and sweetness of old Bill's accordion, imitating calls
of poor, demented creatures while they danced the
      Pride of Erin Waltz.

3

Those men who stand
cutting peat on that headland
watch the cloud of spray
coming from the vessel nearby on the bay,
unaware its presence
might just take their breath away.

4

The surf that reached Garry and Coll
that year was furred with grey pelts, cowls

Much like the ermine clutching the throat
of the Provost's ceremonial cloak he was
    without while stepping on the boat

That day to exchange a word
with those stationed aboard

the *Ben Lomond*, their voices surging like the tide
as nerve and conscience tried its best to hide

knowledge from their visitors that a few
    waves' lengths nearby
creatures crammed in cages had whimpered
    as they died.

A Fishy Story

Once there was a fisherman
who never washed,

whose skin became silver,
voice grew hushed

as sea-winds,
whose consonants were pebbles

collected on the sea-bed,
whose syllables

flowed music on his tongue,
for whom salt became engrained

within bone and muscle, each one
honed by the razor-edge of storms,

his hands and feet mutating into fins,
head and eye transformed

to see through darkness
till mooring lines to land and harbour frayed

and he stepped out into the current
to flick his tail and quickly swim away.

Self-preservation

That fisherman was so often doused in salt
it gave an added savour to his wit
so much so he decided when it came time to slip
the hook he would not be placed with a family vault

Or coffin. Instead he would be dipped
in a barrel over-filled with brine
in order that when the time
for Man was up, his spirit might be tipped

out of that vat in the sure and certain knowledge
his soul and flesh endured
within the sharpness of that pickle –
healed, preserved and cured.

Marilyn Monroe in Stornoway

She should have moved up here.
She'd appreciate how a strong wind might blow,
up and down the Narrows, Bayhead and South Beach,
and how its swirl might puff out skirts, wheech
                               white pants on show
as they did that day her dress
was hitched around her waistline, standing
                                above the grille
of a New York subway. For all an old man
                                 might confess
a sigh of lust, a look up and down that girl
whose flighty ways caused Joe Di Maggio
to throw a jealous punch that evening,
this time there'd be no nasty scenes,
for we'd seen it all before in these parts –
    gusts billowing
    the hemlines
of women walking, every passing Mairi, Sineag,
                              Norma, Jean . . .

Tales My Uncle Told Me

Kyle and Garve and Achnasheen.
Of places where he said he'd been,
magic dwelled in these three names.

Imagined maps of Scotland that
had **'Here Be Mainland'** inked in black
were sketched in my thoughts. Railways trains

Funneled smoke across them – their dark breath
whirling clouds inside my head.
From out of that fog, towns appeared.

Achnasheen prospered. Garve's wide streets
cemented pavements crammed with feet.
Kyle spawned a city. At its piers

Liners harboured. Cranes dipped low
to lift up nest-eggs. People strolled
or rushed to catch a morning bus

Into factories, shopping centres, work.
And later when the skies grew dark,
temptation sparkled – bold and bright and obvious

To one who felt so long confined
to limits islands set on hearts and minds,
and waited for a gangway to be lowered

Between ship and quayside, present and past
to enable my escape. At last,
a thousand frontiers to explore.

Till on that morning the ship's bow
cut through mist and I saw how
wrong my visions had all been.

Gulls mewled round silence. Train stood still.
Some dreams would never be fulfilled
in Kyle or Garve or Achnasheen.

Rudolf Nureyev in Stornoway

He did not hang around here very long.
After Irkutsk and Leningrad, wind whirled him on
far away from Bayhead, that wild boy
who had slipped free of the KGB, the Kirov and Bolshoi

was not going to be restrained by padlocks, chains
elders fastened on the playground swings. He remained
impossible to hold in check, his wayward legs
kicking at the Free kirk pews as he tried to dance there,

perform the plié, the petit saut, and arabesque

Lifting Light

Each arrival brought its miracles.
The *Seaforth* steaming into port,
landing Hillman Hunters, Sunbeams, vehicles
that would speed around our village roads

with number plates and drivers who didn't quite belong.
We watched them touch down – the descent of engines
accompanied by the crank of chains, tintinnabulation,
the thought that something might go wrong,

and there would be a slip of wheels and gears,
a buffeting of wind which would veer and blow
that car sideways, causing it to buck and rear,
toppling and entombing it, without hope of resurrection

within the harbour's murk and foam.

2

The gangway like a ladder clanked in place
to reach the deck
we'd crank our necks
to look at, scan each face

for recognition, to see which friends
might have made the crossing
and come among us, footsteps rocking
down steps to spend time with us again.

Our gaze climbs up that slope and settles
on some relative who gives
a wave and smile, reminder they have lived
for a while among us, before they jostle

with their cases down the steel
steps and we cluster round about them,
delighted that they will
no longer be ghosts, half-lost names among us

but ones whose presence moves and cheers us still.

Flooding

The sea is sometimes too much with us.
In the dark, we can hear it pitch and tilt
within a car-park,
leaving souvenirs of small upheavals
swept up on the Town Hall steps
or draped upon a wall,
both bladderwrack and kelp among its gifts,

and, too, the taste of grit upon our lips,
lodged between teeth and tongue,
the wind that smears
salt upon our faces,
a surge of tears that's somehow
stored within our cheekbones,
sending us its small reminders
of how we do not belong here,

but have only borrowed land
which we shore with cement and tarmac
for fear the Minch will inch back,
reclaiming this great harbour for its own.

Below the Pier

We'd race around the stout legs of the pier,
scaling over flanks and knee-caps, scrambling down
calves and ankles dipped in sea-water,
aware we lay below the dark lap of the town

where parents never pried or peeked, savouring
    light within
that privacy, for all there was the danger we might slip,
become soaked to nerve and skin,
or – worse – be netted by some frogman from a ship

anchored by the pier. Such thoughts seldom troubled.
Instead we out-faced minnows, crabs and eels
congregating near the pier-head, undisturbed
by our proximity, sharing their zeal

for that green harbour, in which rules and real
life could be suspended like our bodies,
the way our limbs flipped and furled
as we sought to master mysteries of this –
    our secret underworld.

Wool-sacks on the Harbour

Near the top of the old fortress,
there stood others; buttresses of wool,
odd-shaped mattresses we could bounce and
    dive upon
during long hours of misrule, playing fool
and endless games of cops'n'robbers
throughout our time out of school.

And they provided, too, a maze that we could
    creep round,
hide and peek, seek ways to dodge the gaze
of passing grown-ups, allow clouds
of wool to muffle sounds of mockery and mayhem
till lorries came down to lift them,
take these sacks up to the tweed-mill
clear away each fleece and clipping that fashioned
    our playground.

A Meeting
(For Iain)

Once when I strolled down the quay in Stornoway,
I met my younger self
swaggering towards me,

scrounging wine off Spanish sailors, obtaining free
cigarettes from fishing-boats,
pressing thumb deep in a beer keg to seek spray

for tongue and lip. I felt embarrassed by him,
preferred not to recall
that he was someone I could ever be,

till I recognised his raucous laughter,
filled with scorn and mockery,
and knew that he directed it

at some old sod like me.

Watching

Distrustful of his wife and sons,
the elder used to take a small collection
of television switches – volume, contrast, off/on –
in his suit pocket to the Sunday sermon,

knowing they would not recognise the error of their ways
and spend their time poisoning eternal souls and gaze
watching *The Onedin Line, When the Boat Comes In* and
    Songs of Praise
within the hours that he was absent upon the Sabbath day.

Instead, those left at home behaved almost as they wished,
stared out the kitchen window, trawled and fished
for talk and gossip, the mesh
of words people flung around that small town

drawing in and netting all of human flesh.

Harbour Worker

When he'd loop and hitch the hawser,
ensuring that the vessel was held tight against the quay,
he'd think of how his father had foreseen
murder in his future. ('*Someday you'll swing free*

above a trapdoor,' he would say,
imagining the temper which his son
sometimes let loose would bring him to a blindfold,
noose, stern punishment for some murderous deed he'd done

to a wife or girlfriend caught in infidelity,
some blow inflicted on a stranger.)
But with the years that threat had passed
and with it, too, the danger

of whoosh and thud, the hangman's rope.
Instead, this daily knot
life fashioned for him each evening
when the ferry sailed to port.

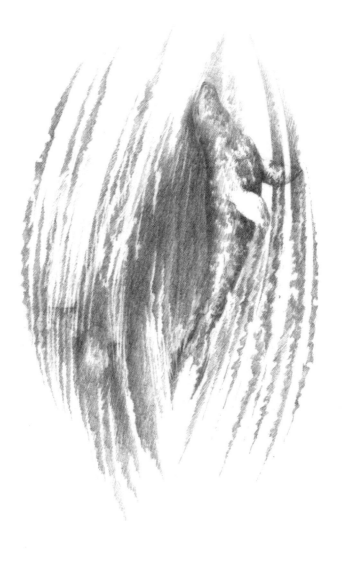

Young Love in Stornoway

We dream of old loves
like the surprise of a seal
rising in the harbour,

that small splash among waves
a recollection of how we used to feel,
the ardour

of that lost presence
a twist of head or tail
before it dips again into the deep

after breaking surface,
leaving no trace of how we failed
to keep

faith in one another,
how trust slipped away
from our command

like that visitor speeding through salt water,
shifting from the shadows, the vague
borders that blur the edge of sea and land.

Old Love in Stornoway

We would often see them.
The old man in his flat cap. Wife with knotted scarf
waiting on King Edward Wharf
for a son or daughter to come home,

the knot between them tight
 – for all it was invisible –
as that thick steel
hawser that tied

the *Suilven* or *Seaforth* to the shore.
Nowadays, we'd envy them, aware
that strong bond's so much rarer
than it was before,

that our frail vessels buck and strain
when settled at the harbour,
that even the clasp of familiar fingers
can sometimes chafe against us like an iron chain.

Love Song with Dogfish

She broke his heart
when she snapped at him last night.

Love Song with Conger Eel

Every night she curled around him.

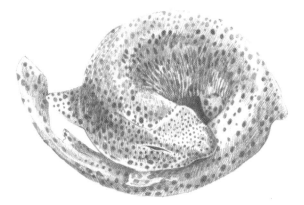

Dockers Strike, 1972

And so it happened that the pubs ran dry of beer,
milk was not splashed on cornflakes; tea
poured out sugarless and brown.
All seemed dry and sour within town
until that day the *Girl Norma* risked seas
to be loaded at the Kyle pier
and bring its welcome cargo here.
Lager for the Carlton. Pints of stout and heavy
for men to wash thirst and sorrow down.
These days barely remembered; dockers now
    rarely found around
the quayside, only the dark dregs of memory
remaining in our glasses after the sup and
    swig of years.

The Girl Who Taught
the Fisherman To Read

The girl who taught the fisherman to read
cut him loose upon a drag and swell of words
as powerful as any that lay siege
to his vessel when a dark storm swayed the world,
as chilling as when a rockpool was disturbed
by a corpse who shared his skills and trade,
    the screech and wings of gulls.

The girl who taught the fisherman to read
made him long to know these letters painted white
on boats tethered at the quayside – 'LK', 'SY', 'PD' –
and find out what careless pleasures these
    consonants might hide
behind each careful brush-stroke. The rocking
    motion of the tide
seemed to promise rhythms he hoped might
    stir his nights.

The girl who taught the fisherman to read
anticipated gratitude and kisses for her time
giving meaning to his harbour – each
chart now understood, each fish-box and warning sign –
only to find out he had slipped her net, their
    lives not now entwined,
and a girl from 'LK', 'SY' or 'PD' has snared
    him on her line.

Love Song without Sole

Life seemed flat without her now.

Love Song with Flounder

He could barely stay upright now she'd gone.

Unlucky Fisherman

I

You could tell the cove was jinxed.
On a dark crag ringed with cuddies,
fish would swim and slink
past his baited hook.

That time, too, a bird,
some cormorant or shag,
gobbled down his line
and he could only look

as its black fins powered
through water into air, nearly took
his feet miles off that rock.
And there was the boat

these weeks they could only net
a galaxy of jelly fish,
haul in their useless violet stars.
They cursed him for a Jonah. Afloat

he seemed only to pluck ill-luck
from the ocean. Until the day they dragged
him from its currents, forced him to stand
where he's been ever after.

Secure and dry on land.

2

When the men strained at the nets,
they were bloated with sea-water,
empty of fish: each barren haul
reminding him of home, the daughter
Mairi had miscarried after months
that small life had been held and stored.
He recalled once again the breakers they rode
together, the cold inside him as the doctor told
them they were unlikely to have children.
It put an end to dreams they'd sailed with all
        those years before.
Some net had frayed within her.
and there would be no life they could succeed in
        bringing safe to shore.

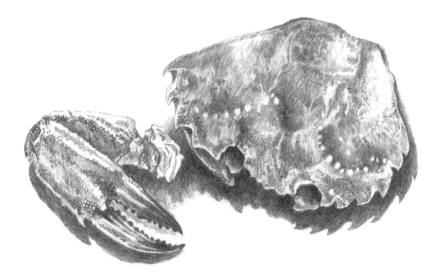

Love Song with Crustaceans

When I saw that crab trapped within the creel,
I recalled how I used to feel
when I first saw you,
heart beating at my rib-cage
or like steel pincers that might claw through
the net life had long reeled tight for me.

Somehow I broke free
and tapped out some mangled message
that you might follow, understand,
allowing you to see
through the shell with which my life had been encased,
all my secrets prised and opened
by the soft touch of your lips, your breath, your hands . . .

Love Song with Seaweed

She fell in love with a man whose hair was the shade of peat
aware that if she went in too deep
too quickly too many of his secrets might just seep
into her soul, becoming conscious too the hold
he placed on her was cloying, that he laid
upon her with the great weight of age,
bearing down with rage that often shuddered through him
till she was anxious to escape the clutch of all that cold.

She next fell for a man whose locks were brown as seaweed,
a tight tangle of kelp or bladderwack,
and she never thought he'd ever slip or slacken,
while his grip tightened within the hush and black
of night, but then a surge swept over him, a pull of tide
unfastening all that held them close and tight together,
as if the seas had sheered them
and washed away his chance of ever rolling back.

She last fell for a man whose eyes were blue or green
depending on how their shade might take the light,
loving to see them alter, how his sight
mirrored the horizons he'd journeyed and seen
throughout his days, the aquamarine
borders of the Caribbean, the darker ebb and flow
of Arctic waters till he settled in this bay with her,
laying down his anchor, never to let go.

Love Song with Mackerel

She bore the stripes of that relationship.

Love Song with Sea Anemone

His heart was full to burst as fishing nets
each night he saw her moving through the dance
inside the hall. A vision in that scarlet dress
pulsing to the rhythm, she made him dream of romance

deep within the darkness till this friend of his declared:
'Keep away from her, cove. She feeds
upon all the tide will spin her way.
Just ignore her beauty. Pay no heed

to that crimson kiss, her bright and frivolous display,
for all who go too close to her, end up as her prey.'

Sealessickness

Upon a beach, the stretch of sand would tilt
and shift in new directions.
The harbour lift, pour silt
dredged from its dark depths upon
the place where he was standing.
Sea-walls moved; piers shifted to prevent
boats from making landing.
There seemed to be no end
to this disease affecting men
like him who'd been at sea too long.
Doctors confined him to the sea-bed till the moment when
the last signs of his symptoms had faded and were gone.

In This Condition

When he found that the tide had just gone out,
he decided to go and drown
himself in long grass within the Castle Grounds,
his body masked by petals, sepals, stamens,
pollen cloaking skin.
It made him think he lay within
deep water, limbs and boles of trees
like seaweed floating free above
the clutch of hands that could not grip
a mast or sail, an anchor-chain or oar,
wake bubbling from the stern of a passing boat or ship.

At the Fish-mart

What was in his head
these mornings that he'd start
the bidding at the fish-mart
was the thought that instead

of selling herring, ling or mackerel
he could somehow obtain
a good price for that offspring who once again
had stumbled, fell

through the door at midnight. In the half-light,
he'd dream someone would shift him from his hands,
call out a loud bid, demand
he'd be lifted from them, that he might

like some spoiled batch of whiting, cod,
be slipped back into the ocean or into the clutch of God.

Selling the Fish at Fish Mart, Stornoway

Leaving

There must be a spell,
some set of magic words,
or an emergency cord
that someone tall enough could rise to pull

(without fear of fine or penalty)
and prevent that vessel,
say, *Seaforth* or *Suilven*, taking its full
quota of exiles out to sea,

for that voyage's been going on too long,
with battered cases in the luggage rack
containing blouses, shirts of those who'll not come back,
the haunted eyes that throng

the bar or crowd the upper deck,
a swirl of Gaelic songs
crooned by those who brood long, hard hours upon
leaving, contemplating the next

stage in their departure,
whether city building sites or quiet nights
of study, these joyless rides
crammed in bus-seats, railway corridors

where they will look up and think to smash
the glass within their carriage that contains
the red dangle of alarm chains,
hoping that the dash

across Minch and mainland might cease,
that brakes could squeal
at the tug of fingers, halt the roll of wave and wheel,
allow those trapped by history

to stay on an island shoreline,
free within its constrained boundaries.

Airnish

A cairn marks out an ebbing tide
where the ragged tatters of a cause
were washed away by scarlet.

A lighthouse beams to guide
ships across that surge of water,
ensuring that their entrance is untroubled, quiet.

And now upon an edge of moorland,
there stands a vast
and iron shed,

Where men set to work with brain and hand
upon steel towers and decks
fashioned to let

Light glow in the future,
harvesting the wind and tide
within the circle of an odd-shaped fishing net.

Love Song with Plankton

His wife had a blaze of freckles on her arm
which he likened to the tiddlers, sprats
he once caught within a schoolboy's fishing-net.
Or the rocks and skerries dotting the sea-chart
that told him he was nearing home
to see her once again, to seek out and explore
the sweet cartography of skin
he studied there, holding to these tiny dots, like spore
between his fingers. These thoughts were what consoled
him when he could only hear the drum of the engine,
knowing he would soon see these specks
swimming like plankton on the surface of her skin.

Love Song with Tropical Fish

Our romance came to an end in the Chinese restaurant.

He kept looking past me, beyond the ring he'd
    slipped upon my hand.

I tried to obtain his attention, demand

his eyes met mine so we could talk about our plans,

but I could tell he was thinking about work again,
    gazing at the fish-tank,

and soon his fingers would be plunged in water,
    trying to bring a more important catch to land.

Fishermen's Mission

When disciples netted souls alongside Christ,
they would not have witnessed scenes like these.
The fisherman with fingers chilled within a
        bag of ice
dangling before him for a surgeon to stitch on.
Crewmen concealed in shadows below the quay.
Exiles huddling for warmth within a van.
Small moments of drama that might cause
        their hearts to freeze
occurring within unfamiliar vessels,
        nylon nets and winching gears.

Yet there's still the grieving widow and the
        orphaned child,
their hearts broken by storms too harsh for them
        to bear,
men with pasts too dark to slip from, their
        futures grim and spoiled,
healing, perhaps, beginning with a trembling
        word of prayer.

A Short Selection of Announcements
Made by Cal Mac about the Failure of Their Vessel
Isle of Lewis To Sail over the Last Few Years

1

The vessel will not sail today
due to a design fault.
It was never built to be
in close contact with salt.

2

The vessel will remain in port
and not leave Stornoway.
Some of the staff have been disturbed
by the presence of a wave.

3

The vessel today will stay in port
and not take to sea.
A leaf has been reported
falling off a tree.

4
(with the assistance of Sheenagh Pugh)

The vessel will not sail today
due to the fact of weather,
a phenomenon never factored in
when they put the ship together.

5
(with the assistance of Guido Blokland)

The vessel will not leave port today
because its decks are full
and weighed down by a shower of rain
leaving Ullapool.

6
(inspired by Stuart Macleod)

The vessel will not sail today,
remaining tied up here
because the captain needed Stevie Wonder's help
to guide it round the pier.

7
(translated into Scots by Doug Robertson)

The vessel will no cast off.
Nae sailing happening the day.
Skipper put his finger oot the windae.
'The wind is blawin' the wrang way!'

8
(written by Angela Smith)

The vessel, it WILL sail today.
It WILL head out to sea,
and Four Horsemen of Apocalypse,
the passengers will be.

Boats

Once they tied their vessels like small, grey mares
with ropes fashioned from heather, horsehair
fastened round rocks or posts embedded in the shore.
No snaffles, bits or reins required. Only a wooden oar
that allowed men to ride slowly out on a trail of waves
into farther, deeper water, sailing to or from that bay.

Now steel is looped round bollards to restrain
the dark bulk of a great horse with a steel throat that contains
cars, container-trucks bearing gifts, full loads
of visitors and home-dwellers who invade the broad roads
of the island, twisting round us like black rope
that knots us all together, each village, bay and slope.

Love Song with Boats

(for Maggie, 10 April 2014)

Small boats in the harbour,
bow and keel lashed together, steel
fastened against steel
so no matter how much either wind or wave might reel,
they can withstand the season's clamour,
their place of safety sealed
by knots hands tied around a bollard,
the tight loop of an iron hawser.

And you and I must be like that,
mimicking the buoyancy of boats
that come together in the shelter of this port,
bound together not by steel or hawser-knot
but by a bond much stronger far than this,
the tie of love that keeps the human heart afloat,
the loop that brings us both together in a kiss.

Valediction

Speedwell, old comrade,
let the wavecrest take you
out of the haunts of darkness
into a brighter morn.

Let a silver cord release you
from these storm-churned channels
into serene waters,
towards a golden dawn.

Fear not in your ocean venture.
A constant friend is with you.
The ripples of past voyages
will – in a little while – be gone,

And with resolve and perseverance,
a flowing stream will bear you
below a glittering constellation
to a peaceful horizon.

Rear View

One of the difficulties in being a writer from a small community is that many are quick to tell you they can spot the original people who feature in your work. They will inform you that they know the individual on whom, say, the figure in 'Sealessickness' is based, having come across some sailor who was sick every time they stepped on shore. While there may or may not be someone just like him, or some of the other eccentric characters who appear in these pages, I assure the reader that they are products purely of my imagination. As a result, I can only offer an apology to those who see similarities between someone they know and those who haunt poems like 'The Girl Who Taught the Fisherman To Read' or 'Love Song with Kippers'. To coin a phrase, any similarities with real people are purely coincidental, and made by the reader's imagination, just as the appearance of the likes of Marilyn Monroe and Bela Lugosi in Stornoway's streets are conjured up by my own.

Yet, to cloud and confuse the issue, there are also many lines of verse in *SY StorY* that are – at least – based on fact. These include a number of the opening poems in the book. There was, for instance, a trio of large stones that guided Mesolithic wanderers' entrance into the bay, situated where they are now. The town also has its roots in a Nordic past and was called *Stjornavager* or 'Steering Bay' at one time. The Fife Adventurers paid the first of two visits to the town in 1598, attempting to colonise the Isle of Lewis for the Scottish Crown. There are also Cromwellian links. Some have suggested that there was a fort at one time on Goat Island in the harbour. However, there appears more likely to have been one in the area bounded by present-day Cromwell Street, North Beach and South Beach. Never one to let the truth (completely) stand in the way of a good story, I have decided to let it be found on Goat Island, home to a boat repair yard today. I hold up my hands, confess my deception here and trust I will be forgiven. This is also the case with the poem, 'Stirrings'. Local legend has it that some of the soil in Stornoway owes much to the ballast brought by foreign boats to the harbour. Whether this is exaggerated or not, I have decided to allow the myth to go unchallenged.

There are other, more factual, poems. 'Foreshores' is about the public wrangling between Sir James Matheson and his wife Lady Mary Jane Matheson, and others over ownership of that stretch of land at the edge of the town. As outlined in Catherine Mackay's more detailed history of the Stornoway Pier and Harbour Commission, this hindered the development of the port for a number of decades, until eventually a solution was found. There are also accounts of various vessels that affected the lives of the people of the town. One is the *Norge*; its sinking off Rockall on 28 June 1904 is one of the most overlooked maritime disasters in this country. Six hundred and forty-five lives were lost. Its 160 survivors, emigrants fleeing Russia and Scandinavia, spent up to eight days in lifeboats before being brought to shore, many being taken to Stornoway. The loss of the *Iolaire* in January 1919 had a devastating effect on particularly the crofting communities of Lewis and Harris for decades, bringing yet more death to many island families after all the trauma and suffering of the First World War. It would take an entire book for anyone to fully explore the effects of that disaster on the people of the island. Its ramifications were still being felt during my teenage years in the town.

There are also tales of emigration. They include the emigrant ship, the *Metagama*, on which many Lewismen rubbed shoulders with Latvians bound for exile in Canada in the 1920s. Another story where the people of the Baltic nations also touched the lives of Lewismen concerns the arrival of two ships, the *Astrid* and the *Ostervag* in 1948. These vessels contained Estonians fleeing Sweden, a country neighbouring the Soviet Union, from the prospect of both the gulag and possible invasion. The fishing boat *Astrid*, with 29 people on board, including 7 children, managed to reach St John's in Newfoundland through the tumultuous seas characteristic of the North Atlantic in late July, an astonishing achievement which impressed anyone who came into contact with those on board. The mayor of St John's, for instance, likened the voyage to those undertaken by Vikings in a past age.

And so it goes on. *Psalm 46* in Gaelic was sung by those gathered in the harbour when the *Loch Ness* took men away from No. 1 Pier in Stornoway on 31 August 1939; the voices of those who had gathered echoing in the stillness, their sound reaching as far as the peninsula of Point. Shoals of herring did not flash their silver tails and fins around the island that year either. Later, in 1952, Stornoway Harbour endured another terrible event connected with war. The waters near Tolsta Head were the venue of both Operation Cauldron and, later, Operation Hesperus; the former taking place on the *Ben Lomond*. This was an experiment involving biological warfare undertaken by scientists from Porton Down, in breach of international law. Rhesus macaque monkeys and guinea pigs were sprayed with a mixture that included both bubonic and pneumonic plague.

More prosaically, it is certainly the case that wool-sacks and beer-kegs were stacked beside the Caledonian MacBrayne building, though the latter disappeared during the year of the dockers' strike. A large grey building was also built in Airnish. For all that it never fulfilled the potential we dreamed of in the early seventies, failing to provide the number of oil-related jobs its sheer scale appeared to promise during these times, it seems to me that this was preferable to the alternative, never to build any structure there at all. Far better to light one candle than . . .

And so to this book, in its own way a lighting of a candle. There are many I would like to thank for their assistance in keeping its flame burning. These include Rev. Donald Michael Macinnes. who provided me with his copy of *Titanic's Predecessor: The Story of the* SS *Norge Disaster of 1904* (Seaward Publishing); the author of that book, Per Kristian Sebak for his meticulous research into that largely forgotten incident; Ross Macleod of 'Back In The Day'; Tonu Orav, Lea Krenin, Maaja Keays, Heikki Vilu, Simpson Buglass, Anna Tucker and the staff at the Estonian Embassy in London for their assistance with the *Astrid* tale; Mary Smith, Angus Murray, Christine MacCuish, Catriona Kennedy, Sandy Matheson, Norman MacArthur, Malcolm Macdonald, Fred Silver, Linda Mackay; Jim Wilkie for his *Metagama* book; John J. Maclennan (the port's former Chief Executive), Catriona Mackay, Angus Smith, Jane Maciver, Magda Choluj and all the staff and board of Stornoway Port Authority who both commissioned this book and assisted me in the undertaking of it; my friend and collaborator Doug Robertson, whose art-work plays no small part in inspiring me; the staff of Birlinn for their unfailing courtesy and professionalism. Finally, my most important debt of gratitude is owed to my wife, Maggie Priest. How any individual can live with a writer is truly beyond my ken.

Donald S. Murray
December 2014